W9-CEN-436

PEARSON

ALWAYS LEARNING

Rachelle Reese

Lab Manual for Database Development

Custom Edition

Cover Art: Courtesy of Kheng Guan Toh/Fotolia, Inc.

Copyright © 2012 by Pearson Learning Solutions

All rights reserved.

Permission in writing must be obtained from the publisher before any part of this work may be reproduced or transmitted in any form or by any means, electronic or mechanical, including photocopying and recording, or by any information storage or retrieval system.

All trademarks, service marks, registered trademarks, and registered service marks are the property of their respective owners and are used herein for identification purposes only.

Pearson Learning Solutions, 501 Boylston Street, Suite 900, Boston, MA 02116
A Pearson Education Company
www.pearsoned.com

Printed in the United States of America

1 2 3 4 5 6 7 8 9 10 VOZN 17 16 15 14 13 12

000200010271310220

JH

ISBN 10: 1-256-74173-6
ISBN 13: 978-1-256-74173-2

BRIEF CONTENTS

CONTENTS

ABOUT THE AUTHOR

Rachelle Reese has been writing programming and database development courses for nearly 20 years. She is an animal lover who lives on a farm with her husband. She is also the co-author of the Dime Store Novel urban fantasy series.

ACKNOWLEDGEMENTS

I'd like to thank my technical review Damian Lai and the team at Pearson for their suggestions and support.

INTRODUCTION

The labs in this manual were designed to be completed on the Virtual Machine DVD that was included with your textbook package. To run the virtual machine, you will need a computer that has VMware Player 3.1.5 (or later). VMware Player can be downloaded free from http://www.vmware.com. The pre-lab explains how to open the virtual machine and should be completed prior to performing the other labs.

Each lab is designated with a group. The Group A labs are based on the Westlake Research Hospital case study. They provide step-by-step instructions to guide you through the tasks being covered. The Group B labs ask you to design and create your own database, based on the requirements defined in the Grandfield College case study. Instead of giving step-by-step instruction, these labs require you to apply the requirements analysis and design skills you have learned. The Group B labs help prepare you for the types of challenges you will face when you work on a project as a database developer or administrator.

Use the Prebuilt Virtual Machine for This Course

These instructions describe how to use the VMware Player to launch the preinstalled virtual machine for the labs in this course:

1. Copy the preinstalled virtual machine onto your USB external pocket hard drive.

   a. Create a folder on your USB portable hard drive to store all the virtual machines used for the curriculum. You may name the folder something like "Virtual Machines for My Courses" and create subfolders in it by the course number.

   b. Create a folder on the external USB hard drive and assign it the name of the course number (PT2520 or IT203).

   c. Put the DVD into the computer and identify all the zipped folders for the virtual machine.

   d. Extract each zipped folder into the virtual machine folder created on the external USB hard drive.

2. Launch the virtual machine in VMware Player.

   a. From the Start button on your desktop, launch VMWare Player as shown below.

b. Click the "Open a Virtual Machine" link.

c. Browse to the folder where you copied the ITT-Lab virtual machine on your USB hard drive and double-click onSQL2008ExpVM.vmx to select it as the virtual machine to open.

3. Once the SQL2008ExpVM virtual machine is ready in the left column, highlight the "PT2520 VM" icon and pull down the "Virtual Machine Settings" menu by clicking the down arrow by Virtual Machine on the top menu bar.

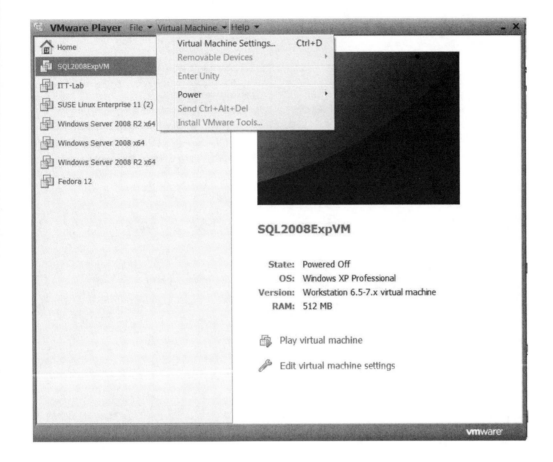

4. Select "Host–only" for the network adaptor and click the OK button to return to the home screen.

5. Double-click SQL2008ExpVM on the left side of the VMware Player
home screen to open the virtual machine. Window XP will start booting.
It might take a few minutes before the virtual machine is fully launched.

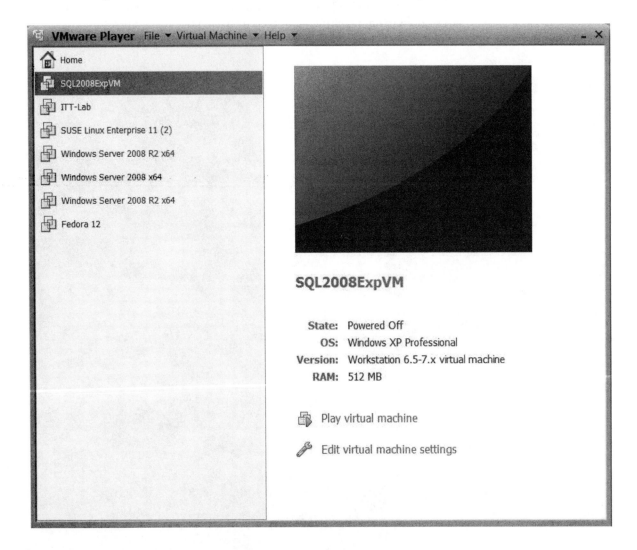

6. This virtual machine is preinstalled with Microsoft SQL Server 2008 Express edition.

IMPORTANT NOTE: Microsoft Visio, required by this course, is NOT part of the virtual machine; you need to switch to the host machine (the lab computer itself) to use all Microsoft Office applications.

7. Shutting down the virtual machine: Like working on any real computer, you must always quit the application programs and shut down the virtual machine properly by clicking on the Start button and selecting the Turn Off option. Wait for the virtual machine to completely power off and the computer returns to the VMware Player home screen.

Do not directly close WMware Player without properly shutting down the virtual machine. Doing so can corrupt your virtual machine and you will lose all the configurations and data that you have saved on the virtual machine.

8. Once the virtual machine is completely powered off, you will arrive back at the VMware Player Menu window, as shown below. Notice that the state of the virtual machine is "Powered Off."

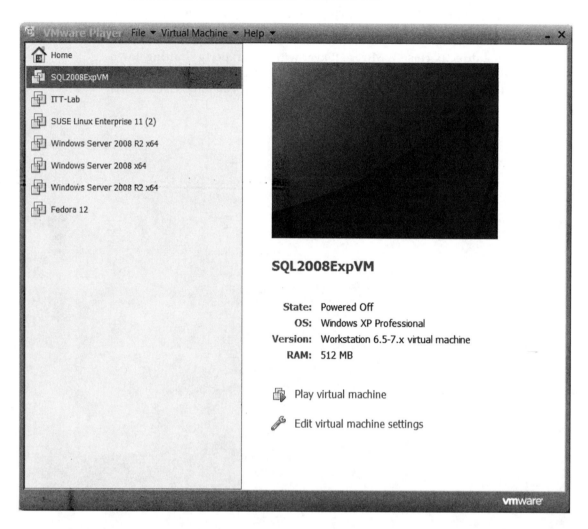

9. Use the in the tool bar of the lab computer to bring up the device menu and double-click to open the removable device icon.

10. Select the drive that is your USB drive to stop it before physically removing it from the computer.

🖨	**Open Devices and Printers**
🖥	UHQ610-000319
	- Eject HL-DT-ST DVD+-RW GT32N ATA Device
💾	Eject External HDD
	- My Passport (F:)
💾	Eject TransMemory
	- TOSHIBA (E:)

Introduction to Databases

This lab accompanies Chapter 1 of Hands-On Database.

Lab 1.1 (Group A)—Explore the AdventureWorks Database Using SQL Server Management Studio

---

Critical Review

- SQL Server 2008 is a relational database.
- A relational database stores information about an entity in a table.
- A piece of information about an entity is called an attribute.
- **Tables are related** to each other through keys.
- **Relational databases** are accessed and modified using Structured Query Language (SQL).

Step 1:Launch the PT2520 virtual machine on your USB drive.

Step 2: Launch SQL Server Management Studio by clicking the **Start** button and choosing **All Programs -> Microsoft SQL Server 2008 -> SQL Server Management Studio**

Step 3: Click the **Connect** button to connect to SQL Server using Windows authentication.

Step 4: Expand **Databases** in the left-hand pane.

Step 5: Expand **AdventureWorks2008** and then expand **Tables**. The AdventureWorks database has a large number of tables. Tables are named using a two-part name. Each two-part table name must be unique. The first part of the name identifies the **schema**, which identifies the context in which the table can be used. For now, think of a schema as a categorization for the table. The second part of the name is the table name.

Step 6: Expand **HumanResources.Employee** and then expand **Columns**.

Step 7: Notice that each column has information after it in parentheses. This information defines, at the very least, the data type that can be stored in the column and whether the column can be empty (null). A column that is "not null" indicates a required piece of information.

Step 8: Expand **Keys**.

```
☐ ▦ HumanResources.Employee
  ☐ 📁 Columns
          🔑 BusinessEntityID (PK, FK, int, not null)
          ▤ NationalIDNumber (nvarchar(15), not null)
          ▤ LoginID (nvarchar(256), not null)
          ▤ OrganizationNode (hierarchyid, null)
          ▤ OrganizationLevel (Computed, smallint, null)
          ▤ JobTitle (nvarchar(50), not null)
          ▤ BirthDate (date, not null)
          ▤ MaritalStatus (nchar(1), not null)
          ▤ Gender (nchar(1), not null)
          ▤ HireDate (date, not null)
          ▤ SalariedFlag (Flag(bit), not null)
          ▤ VacationHours (smallint, not null)
          ▤ SickLeaveHours (smallint, not null)
          ▤ CurrentFlag (Flag(bit), not null)
          ▤ rowguid (uniqueidentifier, not null)
          ▤ ModifiedDate (datetime, not null)
  ☐ 📁 Keys
          🔑 PK_Employee_BusinessEntityID
          🔑 FK_Employee_Person_BusinessEntityID
```

Step 9: There are two keys listed. Both correspond to the same column. The Primary Key (shown in gold) indicates that this is the key you would use to reference a row in the HumanResources.Employee table from a different table. The Foreign Key (shown in silver) references a table where there is information about this entity, which is also shared between other entities. Using keys prevents you from having duplicate information.

Step 10: Double-click **FK_Employee_Person_BusinessEntityID**. Expand the **Tables and Columns** node.

Step 11: Notice that the key FK_Employee_Person_BusinessEntityIDkey relates the BusinessEntityID column of the HumanResources.Employee table to the BusinessEntityID column of the Person.Person table. The other relationships listed in the left-hand pane are foreign keys in other tables that reference the BusinessEntityID column in the HumanResources.Employee table. Click the **Close** Button.

Step 12: **Expand Person.Person** and then expand **Columns**. Notice that the attributes listed here are those that would be applicable to any type of person, not just employees.

Step 13: Right-click **Person.Person** and choose **Select Top 1000 Rows**. You have just executed a Structured Query Language (SQL) query.

Step 14: Close SQL Server Management Studio and power down the virtual machine. You will perform the remaining labs in this unit on the host operating system.

Lab 1.2 (Group A)—Define Major Topics for a Database

Critical Review

- Identifying major topics helps clarify the purpose of a database.
- A good way to start identifying major topics is by interviewing the customer and then listing the nouns.

Step 1: Read the Westlake Research Hospital scenario on p. 18 of the textbook.

Step 2: Create a Word document that contains a table similar to that shown here:

NOUNS	MAJOR TOPIC
hospital	
Doctors	
New Drug	
Prozac	

Step 3: List the nouns in the scenario.

Step 4: Study the nouns and identify which of them are major topics for the database development project.

Step 5: Save the Word document to hand in to instructor at the end of class.

Lab 1.3 (Group B)—Create a Statement of Work

> **Critical Review**
> - A Statement of Work (SOW) is an agreemrnt between you and the customer about what the database project should include and what it should not include. It sets expectations about the timeline and any intermin deliverables.

Step 1: Read the Grandfield College scenario on p. 18 of the textbook.

Step 2: Identify the major topics for this database.

Step 3: Write a draft statement of work that includes the scope, objectives, and a preliminary timeline. You will need to turn in a Word document to the instructor by the end of class.

Lab 1.4 (Group B)—Challenge Activity

> **Critical Review**
> - A flat-file database stores structured data either as delimited data or as fixed-sized blocks.
> - A relational database stores data in related tables.

Step 1: A portion of a flat-file database is shown here.

First Name	Last Name	Address	City	State	Zip code	Birthdate	Renewal date	Amount paid
Joe	Smith	111 Main St.	Sometown	MO	60304	1/2/1973	8/2/2010	200
Tina	Johnson	3203 North St.	Sometown	MO	60304	3/8/1976	9/18/2010	150
Joe	Smith	111 Main St.	Sometown	MO	60304	1/2/1973	8/2/2011	200

1. Describe a situation in which the database might become inconsistent.
2. How could a relational database ensure data consistency?
3. What are some other potential drawbacks to a flat-file database?
4. Explain how you might restructure this data as a relational database.

Step 2: Turn in a Word document with the answers to the questions to the instructor at the end of class.

Gathering Requirements and Business Rules

This lab accompanies Chapters 2 and 3 of *Hands-On Database* textbook.

Lab 2.1 (Group A)—Identify business rules, attributes, and candidate keys

> **Critical Review**
> - Before you begin designing a database, you should gather information using existing forms, interviews, questionnaires, and job shadowing.
> - A business rule describes how data is obtained, processed, or used.
> - A natural key is one based on one or more of an entity's natural attributes.
> - A surrogate key is artificially generated.
> - A composite key is one made up of multiple attributes.

Step 1: Read the Westlake Research Hospital scenario on pages 40-43, and page 59.
Step 2: Study the information in the forms and make a list of questions you would ask.
Step 3: Make a list of business rules and exceptions.
Step 4: You identify a Patient entity and a PatientVisit entity.
    a. Identify the attributes for each entity.
    b. Identify a candidate key for each entity.
    c. Are the keys natural keys, surrogate keys, or composite keys?
    d. Explain why you chose the keys you chose.
Step 5: List some security rules for the database.
Step 6: Turn in a Word document with your answers.

Lab 2.2 (Group B)—Identify entities, attributes, and business rules

> **Critical Review**
> - Data requirements identify the attributes that need to be stored for each entity.
> - Reporting requirements indicate the data that needs to be pulled from the database.
> - Access and security requirements define what actions specific users should be able to perform on the data.

Step 1: Read the Grandfield College scenario on pages 39-40 and 59 of the textbook.

Step 2: Create a Word document.

Step 3: List the data requirements.

Step 4: List the reporting requirements.

Step 5: List the access and security requirements.

Step 6: Make a list of all the nouns related to the requirements.

Step 7: From the list of nouns, identify the entities.

Step 8: For each entity:
  a. Identify the attributes.
  b. Identify a candidate key.

LAB 3

Database Design

This lab accompanies Chapter 4 of the *Hands-On Database* textbook.

Lab 3.1 (Group A)—Complete an Entity Relation Diagram (ERD)

Critical Review

- Before you begin designing a database, you should gather information using existing forms, interviews, questionnaires, and job shadowing.
- An ERD defines entities, attributes, and relationships in a graphical manner.
- In an ERD, entities are represented with rectangles. The entity name is in the top box. The attributes are in rows beneath the entity name. Keys are identified in a column to the left of the attribute name.
- Relationships can be defined with a single headed arrow or using crow feet notation.
- When using a single-headed arrow, it points to the one side of the relationship.
- A lookup entity stores lists that other tables need to look up.
- A linking entity is used to resolve a many-to-many relationship.

Step 1: Read the Westlake Research Hospital scenario on page 79.

Step 2: Launch Visio on your lab computer. Note that Visio is installed on the host operating system, not on your virtual machine.

Step 3: Open Lab3_1starter.vsd. Lab3_1starter.vsd shows a partial database design for the Westlake Research Hospital scenario.

Step 4: Save Lab3_1starter.vsd as nnLab3_1solution.vsd, where nn is your initials.

Step 5: Set the DoctorKey attribute to be the primary key of the Doctors entity.

- Select the **Doctors** entity. The entity's properties are shown below.

Categories:		
⇨ Definition	Physical name:	Doctors
Columns		☑ Sync names when typing
Primary ID	Conceptual name:	Doctors
Indexes		
Triggers	Name space:	
Check		
Extended	Owner:	
Notes		
	Source database:	
	Defining type:	▼

- Click the Primary ID category.
- Select **DoctorKey** and click **Add**. The Doctors entity should look like this:

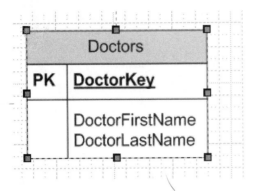

Step 6: Create a one-to-many relationship between the Patients entity and the Doctors entity. Remember, each patient has one doctor, but a doctor can see multiple patients.

- Select the **Patients** entity.
- Click the **Columns** category.
- Add **DoctorKey** as a column.
- Drag a **Relation** object from the **Entity Relationship** pane to the form and connect it to the entities as shown below.

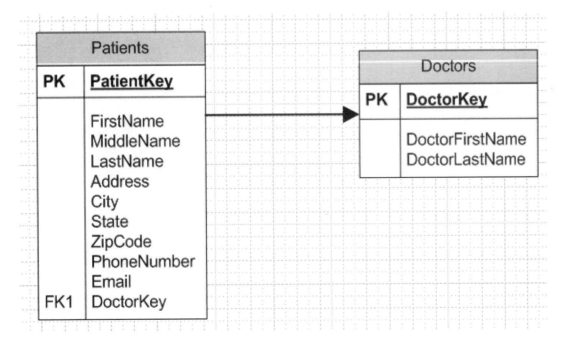

Notice that the **DoctorKey** attribute in the Patients entity is not designated as a foreign key.

Step 7: Change the relationship arrow to display using Crows Feet notation.

- Click the **Database** menu. Point to **Options** and select **Document**.
- Click the **Relationship** tab.
- Check **Crow's Feet**.
- Click **OK**.

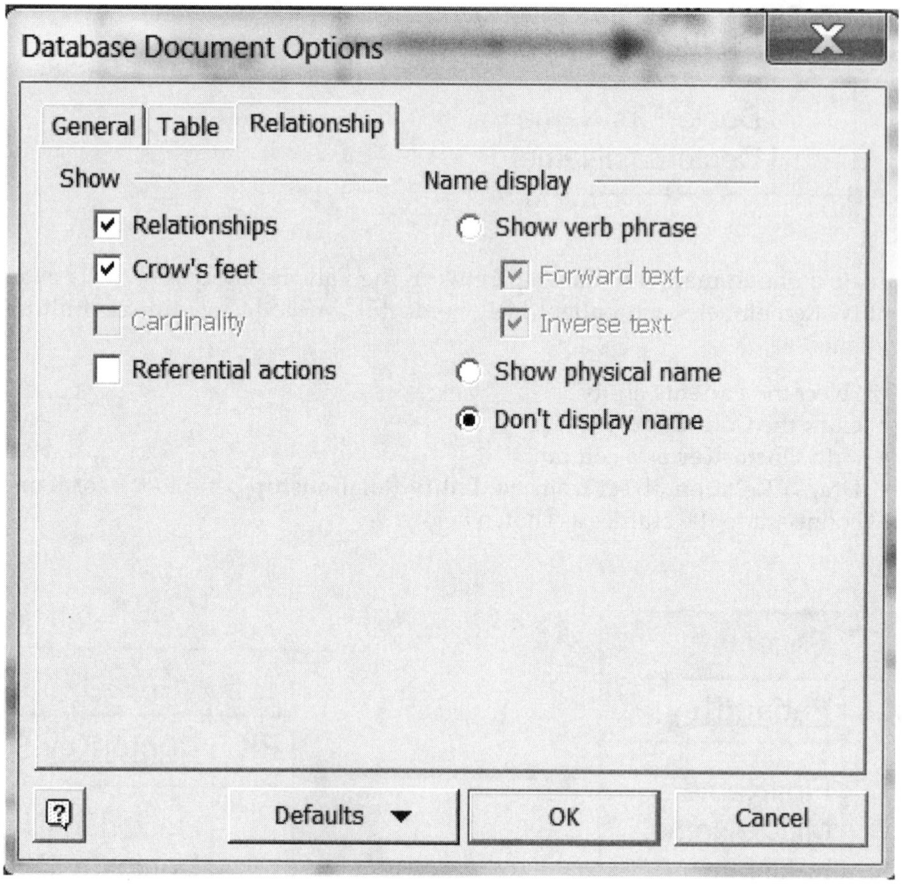

Database Document Options

| General | Table | Relationship |

Show
- ☑ Relationships
- ☑ Crow's feet
- ☐ Cardinality
- ☐ Referential actions

Name display
- ◯ Show verb phrase
  - ☑ Forward text
  - ☑ Inverse text
- ◯ Show physical name
- ◉ Don't display name

Defaults ▼   OK   Cancel

Step 8: Define a one-to-one relationship between the **Patients** entity and the **PatientInitialMedicalHistory** entity. The **PatientKey** attribute should also be the primary key of the **PatientInitialMedicalHistory** entity.

Step 9: Review the Initial Medical History Form on p. 41. Notice that there are two places where medicines are listed. You want the application to be able to provide a list of medicine names the person doing data entry can select from. Each entity that stores a medicine name should do so using a key.

- Modify the current database design so that a medication is only listed in a single entity and then referenced in other tables by a key.
- Add a **PatientMedicationAllergies** entity and define the necessary relationships. Hint: **PatientMedicationAllergies** is a linking entity.
- The completed design should look like this.

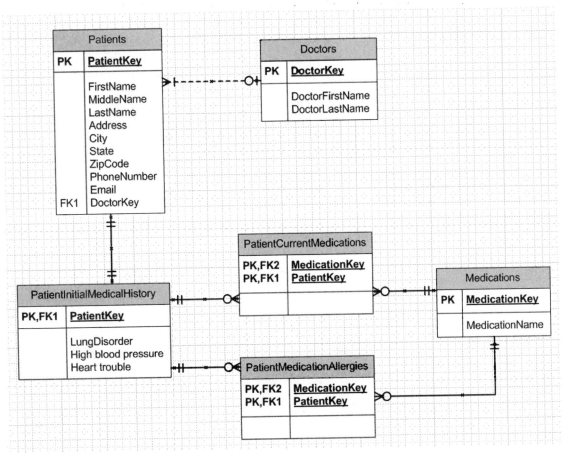

Step 10: Save your changes and submit your .vsd file to your instructor.

Lab 3.2 (Group B)—Design A Database By Visio

Critical Review

- A domain entity is one that is directly related to the purpose of the database.
- A weak entity is one that does not have a meaning, except in the context of another entity.

Step 1: Read the Grandfield College scenario on p. 79 of the textbook.

Step 2: Launch Visio if it is not already open and create a new Database Model Diagram. Save the diagram as nnLab3_2solution.vsd.

Step 3: Add an Entity shape for each domain entity in your database model. Give it a descriptive name.

Step 4: Add attributes to each domain entity. Make sure to define the primary key.

Step 5: Add an Entity shape for any weak entities in your database model.

Step 6: Add attributes to each weak entity. Make sure to define the primary key.

Step 7: Add relations between the weak entities and the domain entity it depends on. Use crow feet notation.

Step 8: Add linking entities to define many-to-many relationships.

Step 9: Add attributes to each linking entity. Make sure to define the primary key.

Step 10: Add relations to define the many-to-many relationships.

Step 11: Save your changes and submit your .vsd file.

Normalization

This lab accompanies Chapter 5 of the *Hands-On Database* textbook.

Lab 4.1 (Group A)—Normalize a Database Design Step-by-Step

Critical Review

- Normalizing a database design eliminates redundancy and helps prevent anomalies.
- To normalize to the First Normal Form:
  - Ensure that each attribute has a single value
  - Remove repeating groups and arrays
  - Ensure that each row is unique
- To normalize to the Second Normal Form:
  - Identify subthemes in an entity
  - Extract the attributes related to subthemes to a separate table
- To normalize to the Third Normal Form:
  - Identify attributes that depend on another attribute for its meaning
  - Extract these attributes to a separate table

Step 1: Read the Westlake Research Hospital scenario on p. 99.

Step 2: Launch Visio on your lab computer. Remember that Visio is installed on the host operating system, not on your virtual machine.

Step 3: Open Lab4_1starter.vsd. Lab4_1starter.vsd shows one table in the database design for the Westlake Research Hospital scenario.

Step 4: Save Lab4_1starter.vsd as nnLab4_1solution.vsd, where nn is your initials.

Step 5: Normalize the PatientVisit table to the first normal form.

- Refer to the Patient Visit form on p. 42 of the textbook. Notice that there are a number of predefined symptoms with checkboxes, as well as a field where the doctor can write symptoms that are not listed. This means that the Symptoms attribute might contain an array of values and violate the first normal form.
- One way to handle this would be to create a separate attribute for each symptom listed, but that still wouldn't handle the possibility that the patient might have other symptoms. Therefore, a better solution is to create a separate entity named PatientVisitSymptoms.
  - Add an entity named PatientVisitSymptoms to the ERD.
  - Define the following attributes:
    - PatientKey (PK)
    - VisitDate (PK)
    - Symptom

- Add a relation that creates a one-to-many relationship between PatientVisit and PatientVisitSymptoms.
    - Remove the Symptoms attribute from the PatientVisit entity.
- Now look at the DoctorNotes attribute. This attribute is one you would want to discuss with the client. If a doctor needs to enter multiple notes, it would be a good idea to normalize using a similar approach as for the Symptoms table. However, if a doctor's note should be treated as a single field, you would want to leave it as it is.

Step 6: Normalize the PatientVisit entity to normal form 2.

- Can you see any functional dependencies in the entity? HINT: Under what circumstance would the DropReason attribute not contain a value?
- Add a DroppedPatient entity that includes the following attributes to your ERD:
    - PatientKey
    - DateDropped
    - ReasonDropped
- Add a one-to-one relationship between the DroppedPatient table and the Patient table.
- Remove the ContinueOrDrop and DropReason attributes from the Patient Visit table.

Step 7: Normalize the PatientVisit entity to normal form 3.

- Are there attributes that do not relate to the primary key? What about DoctorName? Remember, each patient is assigned a doctor, which is identified by DoctorKey in the Patients entity. Therefore, DoctorName is dependent on only PART of the primary key, not on the full primary key.
- Remove the DoctorName attribute from the PatientVisit entity.

Step 8: Your normalized table should look like this:

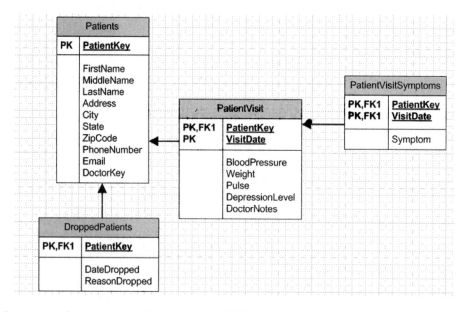

Step 9: Save your changes and submit your .vsd file to your instructor.

Lab 4.2 (Group B)—Normalize a Database

> **Critical Review**
> ▪ Normalizing a database design eliminates redundancy and helps prevent anomalies.
> ▪ To normalize to the First Normal Form:
>   • Ensure that each attribute has a single value
>   • Remove repeating groups and arrays
>   • Ensure that each row is unique
> ▪ To normalize to the Second Normal Form:
>   • Identify subthemes in an entity
>   • Extract the attributes related to subthemes to a separate table
> ▪ To normalize to the Third Normal Form:
>   • Identify attributes that depend on another attribute for its meaning
>   • Extract these attributes to a separate table

Step 1: Read the Grandfield College scenario on p. 99 of the textbook.

Step 2: Launch Visio if not already open and the database design you saved in Unit 3 (nnLab3_2solution.vsd). Save the diagram as nnLab4_2solution.vsd.

Step 3: Normalize your database design to the First Normal Form.

Step 4: Normalize your database design to the Second Normal Form.

Step 5: Normalize your database design to the Third Normal Form.

Step 6: Review your design. Here are some questions to ask yourself:

- Are there any attributes that contain more than one value?
- Can each row in each table be uniquely identified?
- If Windows Vista was installed, uninstalled, and then installed again on the same computer, would the data in the database be accurate?
- If a user requested software that did not have available licenses, but later the licenses became available, would the database be able to track the history of the request?
- If a software vendor is bought out or changes its name, how easy will it be to modify the data in the database?

Step 7: Ask a classmate to look over your design and identify possible insertion, update, or deletion anomalies.

Step 8: Save your changes and submit your .vsd file to your instructor.

Physical Design

This lab accompanies Chapter 6 of *Hands-On Database*.

Lab 5.1 (Group A)—Create a Database Step by Step

Step 1: Read the Westlake Research Hospital scenario on page 122 of your textbook. In this lab, you will be implementing the portion of the database shown in the ERD.

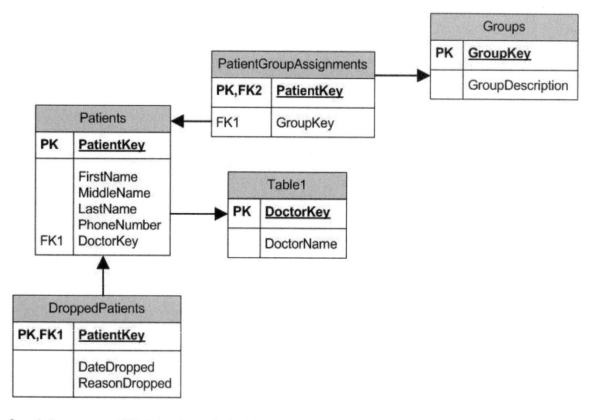

Step 2: Insert your USB drive. Launch the VMware Player.
Step 3: Play the SQL2008ExpVM virtual machine stored on your USB drive.
Step 4: Click **Start** and choose **SQL Server Management Studio**.
Step 5: Click **Connect**.

Step 6: Right-click **Database** and choose **New Database**.
Step 7: Type **Westlake** in the **Name** field and click **OK**.
Step 8: Expand **Databases**. The Westlake database should be shown.

Step 9: Expand **Westlake** and select **Tables**.
Step 10: Create the Doctors table by following these steps:

- Right-click **Tables** and choose **New Table**.
- Type **DoctorKey** in the **Column Name** field,
- Select **nchar** in the **Data type** field. Replace **10** with **15** to create a 15-character fixed-length column.
- Clear the **Allow Nulls** checkbox
- Right-click **DoctorKey** and choose **Set Primary Key**.
- Type **DoctorName** in the **Column Name** field.
- Clear the **Allow Nulls** checkbox.
- Select **varchar** in the **Data type** field and keep the default maximum size of 50. The table specification should look like this:

Column Name	Data Type	Allow Nulls
DoctorKey	nchar(15)	☐
DoctorName	varchar(50)	☐
		☐

- Click File -> Save Table_1.
- When prompted for the table name, type Doctors and click OK.

Step 11: Create the Patients table to match the one shown here:

Column Name	Data Type	Allow Nulls
PatientKey	nchar(15)	☐
DoctorKey	nchar(15)	☐
FirstName	varchar(25)	☐
MiddleName	varchar(25)	☑
LastName	varchar(25)	☐
PhoneNumber	nchar(20)	☑
		☐

ITT-240DD1425... dbo.Table_2*   *ITT-240DD1425... - dbo.Table_1*

Step 12: Create the DroppedPatients table to match the one shown here:

Column Name	Data Type	Allow Nulls
PatientKey	nchar(15)	☐
DateDropped	date	☐
ReasonDropped	varchar(200)	☐
		☐

Step 13: Create the Groups table using the CREATE TABLE statement.

- Click the **New Query** button.
- Type the following in the query window:

```
CREATETABLE Groups

(

GroupKey nchar(5) PRIMARYKEY,

GroupDescription varchar(50) NOTNULL

)
```

- Click **Query -> Execute**.

Step 14: Create the PatientGroups table using the CREATE TABLE statement. HINT: Make sure to match the PatientKey and GroupKey data types with those used in the Patients and Groups tables.

Step 15: Create relationships.

- Expand **DatabaseDiagrams**.
- When prompted to create objects, click **Yes**.
- Right-click **DatabaseDiagrams** and choose **NewDatabaseDiagram**.
- Select each table and click **Add**.
- Arrange the tables so that they look like this:

PatientGroups		Groups	
GroupKey		♀ GroupKey	
♀ PatientKey		GroupDescription	

Patients	
♀ PatientKey	
DoctorKey	
FirstName	
MiddleName	
LastName	
PhoneNumber	

Doctors *	
♀ DoctorKey	
DoctorName	

DroppedPatients	
♀ PatientKey	
DateDropped	
ReasonDropped	

- Click the **DoctorKey** column in the **Doctors** table and drag to the **Patients** table. The following dialog should be displayed:

Tables and Columns   ? X

Relationship name:

FK_Patients_Doctors

Primary key table:	Foreign key table:
Doctors	Patients
DoctorKey	DoctorKey

OK   Cancel

- Click **OK**.
- Click **OK**.
- Use the same procedure to establish the rest of the relationships. For each, make sure the primary key table and column and foreign key table and column are correct before clicking **OK**. TIP: You can delete a relationship by right-clicking it and choose **Delete Relationship from Database**. You can edit a relationship's tables and columns by selecting the relationship, expanding **Tables and Columns Specification**, and clicking the button next to **Tables and Columns Specification**.

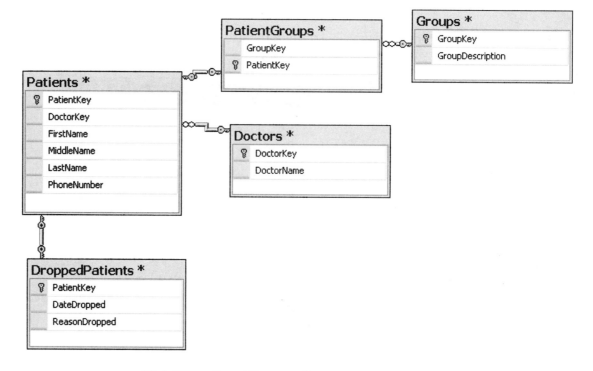

- Your completed diagram should look like this:

- Click **File -> Save Diagram_0**.
- Name the diagram *nn*Lab5-1.
- When prompted to save tables, click **Yes**.

Step 16: Add test data to the database.

- Right-click **dbo.Doctors** and choose **Edit Top 200 Rows**.
- Enter the following test data:

DoctorKey	DoctorName
123	Jones
456	Smith
11111	Thomas
22222	Wong

- Click the Close (x) button.
- Enter the following data in the Patients table:

ITT-240DD1425... dbo.Patients

PatientKey	DoctorKey	FirstName	MiddleName	LastName	PhoneNumber
1-24	123	Sally	Lee	Johnson	555-1212
5-13	456	Mike	NULL	Samuels	555-8923
4-15	123	George	NULL	Martinez	555-3333
NULL	NULL	NULL	NULL	NULL	NULL

- Enter the following data in the Groups table:

ITT-240DD1425... - dbo.Groups

GroupKey	GroupDescription
1	Prozac
2	Experimental
NULL	NULL

- Enter the following data in the PatientGroups table:

ITT-240DD1425....PatientGroups

GroupKey	PatientKey
1	1-24
1	5-13
2	4-15

- Enter the following data in the DroppedPatients table:

ITT-240DD142...oppedPatients

PatientKey	DateDropped	ReasonDropped
4-15	2012-01-02	High blood pressure
NULL	NULL	NULL

Step 17: Save and submit a file that shows your work.

- Take a screenshot of your **DatabaseDiagram**.
- Right-click the Westlake database.
- Choose **Script Database As -> CREATE TO -> File**.
- Save your file as nnLab5-1.sql and copy it to your USB drive.
- Submit both the screenshot and the .sql file to your instructor at the end of class.

Lab 5.2 (Group B)—Create a Database

Step 1:   Read the Grandfield College scenario on p. 122 of the textbook.

Step 2:   Create a database named GrandfieldCollege.

Step 3:   Study the ERD you normalized in Lab 4.2. Choose the appropriate data type for each attribute and determine whether the column should allow nulls.

Step 4:   Create the tables.

Step 5:   Create the relationships.

Step 6:   Populate the database with some test data.

Step 7:   Submit a screenshot of the database to your instructor at the end of class.

SQL Queries I

This lab accompanies Chapter 7 of *Hands-On Database*, pp. 123-139.

Lab 6.1 (Group A)—Writing SELECT Statements

Step 1: Launch the VMware Player and play the SQL2008ExpVMvirtual machine stored on your USB drive.

Step 2: Open a Word document on the host computer and save it as *nn*Lab6-1answers. You will be asked questions during this lab and document the answers in the Word document. This is the file you will turn in to your instructor.

Step 3: On the virtual machine, open SQL Server Management Studio and connect to the SQL Server Express instance.

Step 4: Right-click the Westlake database and click **New Query**.

Step 5: Execute queries to retrieve information from the Westlake database.

1. Type the following query and then click **Query -> Execute**

   ```
   SELECT*FROM Doctors
   ```

   Question 1: How many rows were returned?

   Question 2: How many columns were returned?

2. Type and execute a query that returns all rows and columns of the Patients table.

   Question 3: What query did you execute?

3. Execute a query that returns only the FirstName, LastName, and PhoneNumber columns of the Patients table.

   Question 4: Which query did you execute?

4. Execute a query that returns the LastName of only the patients that have a DoctorKey column of 123.

   Question 5: Which query did you execute?

5. Execute the following query:

```
SELECT Count(*) FROM Patients WHERE DoctorKey = '123
```

Question 6: What did this query tell you?

6. Execute the following query:

```
SELECT FirstName + ' ' + LastName + ' ' AS Patient
FROM Patients
```

Question 7: How many rows were returned?

Question 8: How many columns were returned?

7. Execute the following query:

```
SELECT * FROM Patients
WHERE MiddleName IS NULL OR FirstName = 'George'
```

You can use IS NULL and IS NOT NULL to check whether a column that allows nulls contains a value or null.

8. Right-click the **AdventureWorks** database and choose **New Query**.

9. Execute the following query:

```
SELECT * FROM HumanResources.Employee WHERE VacationHours> 0 AND
SalariedFlag = 1
```

Question 9: Assuming that a value of 1 in the SalariedFlag column indicates a salaried employee, what did this query tell you?

Question 10: How many rows were returned?

10. Execute a query that returns a list of employees who have either vacation hours or sick leave. *HINT:* Use the OR operator.

Question 11: What query did you execute?

11. Execute the following query:

```
SELECT* FROM HumanResources.Employee
WHERE VacationHours BETWEEN 40 AND 80
```

Question 12: How many rows were returned?

12. Modify the query to return the same data as in step 11, sorted by vacation hours in descending order.

Question 13: What did you add to the query?

13. Execute the following query:

```
SELECT COUNT(*) FROM HumanResources.Employee
WHERE OrganizationLevel = 2
```

Question 14: What value was returned?

14. Execute the following query:

```
SELECT SUM(VacationHours) AS TotalVacationHours
FROM HumanResources.Employee
```

Question 15: What value was returned?

15. Execute the following query:

```
SELECT OrganizationLevel, SUM(VacationHours) AS TotalVacationHours
FROM HumanResources.Employee
GROUP BY OrganizationLevel
```

Question 16: What did this query tell you?

16. Write a query that returns the average, most, and least vacation hours, formatted as shown here:

	Average	Most	Least
1	50	99	0

Question 17: Which query did you use?

17. Execute the following query:

```
SELECT*FROM HumanResources.Employee
WHERE BirthDate LIKE '1959%'
```

Question 18: How many rows were returned?

18. Execute a query that returns all employees with a title that begins with "Research."

   Question 19: What query did you use?

19. Execute the following query:

```
SELECT LoginID, VacationHours + SickLeaveHours AS 'Hours Owec
FROM HumanResources.Employee
```

   Question 20: How would you change the query to determine which employee has the highest number of vacation hours and sick leave hours?

Lab 6.2 (Group B)—Write Queries to Meet Business Requirements

Step 1: Review the Grandfield College scenario, particularly the information given on pages 18 and 39-40 of the textbook.

Step 2: Create a Word document.

Step 3: Write queries to address the following business requirements. Test each query using SQL Server Management Studio. Add more data to the database if necessary to test the query.

NOTE: As you work through the queries, you might find that you need to change your database design to meet the business requirements. Go ahead and make any necessary changes.

After the query is working, copy it to the Word document.

1. Generate a list of all software requests.
2. Generate a list of all pending software requests.
3. Generate a report of all responses to a specific request.
4. Generate a report that shows a list of computers where a specific application is installed.
5. Generate a report that returns all installed software products that include the word "Office".
6. Generate a report that returns all software products that include the word "Office" or have Microsoft as the vendor.
7. Generate a report that shows the number of installed copies, grouped by software key.
8. Generate a list of licenses that are past the end date.
9. Execute a query that returns the number of licenses that are past the end date.
10. Generate a report that shows the maximum, minimum, and average price of a license.

Step 4: Submit the Word document to your instructor at the end of class.

SQL Queries II

This lab accompanies Chapter 8 of *Hands-On Database*, pp. 139-150 and Chapter 4 of *Microsoft SQL Server 2008 Management and Administration*, pp. 161-168.

Lab 7.1 (Group A)—Writing Queries to Modify and Join Data

Critical Review
- Use a JOIN to retrieve data from multiple related tables.
- INNER JOIN—returns only rows that have a matching key in both tables
- LEFT JOIN and RIGHT JOIN—returns all the rows of one table and the related rows in the other table.
- Use an INSERT statement to add a row to a table.
- Use an UPDATE statement to modify one or more rows in a table.
- Use a DELETE statement to delete one or more rows from a table.
- Use a TRIGGER to cause an action to occur instead of, before, or after an INSERT, UPDATE, or DELETE.
- Create indexes to optimize frequent queries.
- A clustered index determines the way the table is sorted on the disk.
- A nonclustered index creates a b-tree structure used to search for data.

Step 1: Launch the VMware Player and play the SQL2008ExpVM virtual machine stored on your USB drive.

Step 2: Open a Word document on the host computer and save it as *nn*Lab7-1answers. You will be asked questions during this lab and document the answers in the Word document. This is the file you will turn in to your instructor.

Step 3: On the virtual machine, open SQL Server Management Studio and connect to the SQL Server Express instance.

Step 4: Right-click the Westlake database and click **New Query**.

Step 5: Execute queries to retrieve information from the Westlake database.

1. Type the following query and then click **Query -> Execute**

```
INSERT INTO Patients
(PatientKey, DoctorKey, FirstName, MiddleName, LastName,
PhoneNumber)VALUES ('2-3','22222','Susan',NULL,'Michaels','555-
4444')
```

Question 1: How many rows were affected?

2. Issue a SELECT statement to test your INSERT.
Question 2: How many rows were returned?

3. Execute a query that assigns Susan Michaels to the Experimental group.
Question 3: What query did you execute?

4. Execute the following query:
```
UPDATE Patients
SET DoctorKey ='123'
WHERE PatientKey ='2-3'
```
Question 4: How many rows were affected?

5. Execute a query that assigns all patients currently assigned to Dr. Jones to Dr. Thomas.
Question 5: Which query did you execute?

Question 6: How many rows were affected?

6. Execute the following query:
```
SELECT FirstName +' '+ LastName +' 'AS Patient,
DoctorName AS Doctor
FROM Patients
JOIN Doctors ON Patients.DoctorKey = Doctors.DoctorKey
```
Question 7: How many rows were returned?

7. Execute the following query:
```
SELECT FirstName +' '+ LastName +' 'AS Patient,
DoctorName AS Doctor
FROM Patients
RIGHT JOIN Doctors ON Patients.DoctorKey = Doctors.DoctorKey
```
Question 8: How many rows were returned? Explain why.

8. Execute the following query:

```
SELECT FirstName +' '+ LastName +' 'AS Patient,
DoctorName AS Doctor
FROM Patients
RIGHT JOIN Doctors ON Patients.DoctorKey = Doctors.DoctorKey
JOIN PatientGroups ON PatientGroups.PatientKey =
Patients.PatientKey
WHERE GroupKey=1
```

Question 9: How many rows were returned?

9. Execute the following query:

```
SELECT COUNT(*)As Patients,
DoctorName AS Doctor
FROM Patients
RIGHTJOIN Doctors ON Patients.DoctorKey = Doctors.DoctorKey
JOIN PatientGroups ON PatientGroups.PatientKey =
Patients.PatientKey
GROUP BY Doctors.DoctorName
```

Question 10: What information did you learn?

10. Execute the following query:

```
CREATE TRIGGER trgDropPatient ON Patients INSTEAD OF DELETE
AS
DECLARE @Patient NCHAR(15)
SELECT @Patient = PatientKey From Deleted
INSERT INTO DroppedPatients(PatientKey, DateDropped, ReasonDropped)
VALUES (@Patient,GetDate(),'Attempted deletion')
```

11. Expand the Triggers folder under the Patients table.

12. Test the trigger by executing the following statement:

```
DELETE FROM Patients WHERE PatientKey ='2-3'
```

13. Execute a SELECT statement to show all rows of the Patients table.

Question 11: Is Patient 2-3 still listed?

14. Execute a SELECT statement to show all the names of all dropped patients and the date they were dropped.

15. Take a screenshot that shows the results of the SELECT statement and the expanded Triggers folder.

Lab 7.2 (Group B)—Write Queries to Meet Business Requirements

> **Critical Review**
> ▪ One of the primary jobs of a database developer is writing queries that retrieve the information needed by a business.
> ▪ Test each query to make sure it accurately retrieves the data needed.

Step 1: Review the Grandfield College scenario, particularly the information given on pages 18 and 39-40 of the textbook.

Step 2: Create a Word document.

Step 3: Write queries to address the following business requirements. Test each query using SQL Server Management Studio. Add more data to the database if necessary to test the query.

NOTE: As you work through the queries, you might find that you need to change your database design to meet the business requirements. Go ahead and make any necessary changes.
After the query is working, copy it to the Word document.

- Generate a list of computers where software is installed that has a license that is past its end date.
- Write a trigger that prevents a user from deleting a row in the InstalledSoftware table and instead records the fact that the software has been uninstalled and the current date.
- Test your trigger.
- Open your trigger and take a screenshot to turn in to your instructor.
- Write queries to perform the following tasks. After testing each query, copy it to a Word document.
  - Insert a row that records a software installation.
  - Insert a request for new software.
  - Enter a response to a software request.
  - Change the value in a field that identifies the location of a specific computer.
  - Change the status of a software request to Approved.

Step 4: Submit the Word document and your screenshot.

Database Security I

This lab accompanies Chapter 8 of *Hands-On Database* and Chapter 7 of *Microsoft SQL Server 2008 Management and Administration*.

Lab 8.1 (Group A)—Implement Authentication, Authorization, Views, Stored Procedures, and Backup

Critical Review
- Create a login to allow a user to be authenticated.
- Create a role to grant permission to specific database objects.
- Create a view to restrict the columns or rows retrieved by a user.
- Create a stored procedure to control which data is returned programmatically.
- A full backup backs up the entire database.
- A transaction log backup backs up only the transaction log.

Step 1: Launch the VMware Player and play the SQL2008ExpVM virtual machine stored on your USB drive.

Step 2: Open a Word document on the host computer and save it as *nn*Lab8-1answers. You will be asked questions during this lab and document the answers in the Word document. This is the file you will turn in to your instructor.

Step 3: On the virtual machine, open SQL Server Management Studio and connect to the SQL Server Express instance.

Step 4: Re-read the Westlake Research Hospital case study on page 18 of the textbook. The case study identifies three types of users:

- Doctors
- Patients
- Researchers

Create a table like the one shown below for each type of user and document the access required.

TABLE	SELECT	INSERT	UPDATE	DELETE	COMMENTS
Patients					
Doctors					
Patient Visits					
Patient Groups					
Dropped Patients					

Step 5: Create logins.

1. Click **New Query** on the toolbar.

2. Execute the following:

```
use master
```

3. Execute the following statement:

```
CREATE LOGIN DoctorLogin WITH PASSWORD='P@ssw0rd',
DEFAULT_DATABASE= Westlake
```

4. Execute a statement that creates a login named PatientLogin with the password 'PatientP@ssword2' and sets the default database to Westlake.
   Question 1: Which statement did you use?

5. Execute a statement that creates a login named ResearchLogin with the password 'Re-5earch' and sets the default database to Westlake.

Step 6: Create roles and assign members.

1. Right-click Westlake and choose **New Query**.

2. Execute the following statement:

```
CREATE ROLE DoctorRole
```

3. Execute the following statement to create a user named DoctorUser:

```
CREATE USER DoctorUser FOR LOGIN DoctorLogin
```

4. Execute the following system stored procedure to add DoctorLogin to DoctorRole:

```
EXEC sys.sp_addrolememberDoctorRole, DoctorUser
```

5. Repeat Steps 1-4 to configure users and roles for patients and researchers.
   TIP: For each statement, substitute "Doctor" with "Patient" or "Research."

Step 7: Neither patients nor doctors are allowed to view which group a patient belongs to. Grant Researchers the SELECT permission on the PatientGroups table.

1. Execute the following statement:

   ```
   GRANT SELECT on vw_PatientGroups To ResearchRole
   ```

2. Execute a statement to grant INSERT permission on PatientGroups to ResearchRole.

3. Click **Query -> Connection -> Change Connection**.

4. Select **SQL Server Authentication**.

5. Type **ResearchLogin** as the user and **Re-5earch** as the password. Click **Connect**.

6. Execute the following query:

   ```
   SELECT * FROM PatientGroups
   ```

   Question 2: What happened? *Permission denied.*

7. Execute the following query:

   ```
   UPDATE PatientGroups SETGroupKey= 2 WHEREPatientKey='1-24'
   ```

   Question 3: What happened and why? *Permission denied schema 'dbo'*

Step 8: Create views.

1. Right-click the Patients table. Choose **Script Table As -> SELECT to -> New Query Editor Window**.

2. Above the SELECT clause, type the following:

   ```
   CREATE VIEW vw_Patients
   AS
   ```

3. Execute the query.

4. Expand the **Views** folder in **Object Explorer** to verify that the view was created.

5. Create a view named vw_PatientDoctor that includes the doctor's last name instead of the DoctorKey field. Use an alias of Doctor to identify the column. Hint: Use an INNER JOIN.

6. Execute a SELECT statement on vw_PatientDoctor to verify the results.

   Question 4: How many rows were returned? *4 Rows.*

Step 9: Grant permission on vw_PatientDoctor.

1. Execute the following statement:

   ```
   GRANT SELECT ON vw_PatientDoctor TO DoctorRole
   ```

2. Grant the SELECT privilege on vw_PatientDoctor to PatientRole.

3. Reconnect as DoctorUser to verify that you can select data from vw_PatientDoctor.

4. Reconnect as PatientUser to verify that you can select data from vw_PatientDoctor.

Step 10: Create a stored procedure that returns all patients.

1. Reconnect using Windows authentication.

2. Execute the following statement:

```
CREATE PROC usp_GetAllPatients

AS

SELECT*FROMPatients
```

3. Execute the following statement:

```
EXEC usp_GetAllPatients
```

Step 11: Create a stored procedure that accepts the DoctorKey as a parameter and retrieves a list of all patients for that doctor.

1. Execute the following statement:

```
CREATE PROCEDURE usp_GetDoctorPatients

@DoctorKey nchar(15)

AS

SELECT*FROM Patients WHERE DoctorKey = @DoctorKey
```

2. Execute the following query:

```
usp_GetDoctorPatients 11111
```

Step 12: Now create a stored procedure that uses the vw_PatientDoctor view to retrieve the patients for a specific doctor. Remember, vw_PatientDoctor stores the doctor's name in the Doctor field instead of the doctor key. Therefore, you will need to declare a variable that will store the doctor's name and use that variable in the SELECT statement that retrieves the data from the view.

1. Execute the following statement:

```
CREATE PROCEDURE usp_GetMyPatients

@DoctorKey nchar(15)

AS

DECLARE @DoctorName varchar(50)

SELECT @DoctorName = DoctorName FROM Doctors

WHERE DoctorKey = @DoctorKey

SELECT*FROM vw_PatientDoctor WHERE Doctor = @DoctorName
```

2. Execute the following query:

```
usp_GetMyPatients 11111
```

Question 5: Which rows were returned?

Step 13: Grant permission on usp_GetMyPatients and test.

1. Grant the EXECUTE permission to the DoctorRole.

2. Reconnect as DoctorUser.

3. Execute the query:

```
usp_GetMyPatients 11111
```

Step 14: Back up the database.

1. Reconnect using Windows Authentication.

2. Execute the following statement:

```
BACKUP DATABASE Westlake
TODISK=N'C:\nnLab8-1.bak'
```

3. Copy the backup file to your USB drive and submit along with your Word document.

Lab 8.2 (Group B)—Implement Authentication, Authorization, Views, Stored Procedures, and Backup

> **Critical Review**
> ▪ Create a login to allow a user to be authenticated.
> ▪ Create a role to grant permission to specific database objects.
> ▪ Create a view to restrict the columns or rows retrieved by a user.
> ▪ Create a stored procedure to control which data is returned programmatically.
> ▪ A full backup backs up the entire database.
> ▪ A transaction log backup backs up only the transaction log.

Step 1: Review the Grandfield College scenario, particularly the information given on pages 18 and 39-40 of the textbook.

Step 2: Create a Word document.

Step 3: Create tables that define the access required for the database.

Step 4: Create the logins, users, and roles.

Step 5: Create at least one view and grant the necessary permissions.

Step 6: Back up your database and submit the backup file along with the Word document.

Database Security II

This lab accompanies Chapter 8 (pages 316-331)and Chapter 9 of *Microsoft SQL Server 2008 Management and Administration*.

Lab 9.1 (Group A)—Harden SQL Server and a database

> **Critical Review**
> - SQL Server supports two types of authentication: Windows authentication and SQL Server authentication.
> - Windows authentication associates a SQL Server login with a Windows user account.
> - When using SQL Server authentication, it is a good idea to disable or change the name of the sa account.
> - You can use server-level roles to assign permission to perform server administration tasks.
> - You can use fixed database-level roles to assign permissions to administer and access a database.
> - You can use the ALTER LOGIN statement to modify a login or unlock a locked login.
> - You can create an application role that is not associated with a specific database user.

Step 1: Launch the VMware Player and play the SQL2008ExpVM virtual machine stored on your USB drive.

Step 2: Open a Word document on the host computer and save it as *nn*Lab9-1answers. You will be asked questions during this lab and document the answers in the Word document. This is the file you will turn in to your instructor.

Step 3: On the virtual machine, open SQL Server Management Studio and connect to the SQL Server Express instance.

Step 4: View authentication settings.

1. Right-click the instance of SQL Server Express and click **Properties**.
2. Click **Security**.

   Question 1: Which authentication mode is enabled?

3. Click **OK**.

Step 5: Create a login and grant add it to the sysadmin server-level role.

1. Click **New Query**.

2. Make sure **master** is selected as the database.

3. Execute the following statement:

```
CREATE LOGIN secretAdmin WITH PASSWORD='&dm1n'
```

4. Execute the following statement:

```
sp_addsrvrolemember'secretAdmin','sysadmin'
```

Step 6: Rename and disable the sa account.

1. Execute the following statement:

```
ALTER LOGIN sa DISABLE
```

2. Execute the following statement:

```
ALTER LOGIN sa WITH NAME = [Hidden Account]
```

3. Expand the **Security** node.

4. Expand the **Logins** node.

5. If your changes are not shown, click the **Refresh** button.

6. Take a screenshot and save it as nnLab9-1Step6 to turn in along with your Word document.

Step 7: Create and test an applicaton role name PatientDataRole in the Westlake database. Assign the password P@t1ent.

1. Expand **Databases**.

2. Right-click the **Westlake** database and choose **New Query**.

3. Execute the following statement:

```
CREATE APPLICATION ROLE PatientDataRol
WITH PASSWORD='P@t1ent'
```

4. Execute the following statement:

```
GRANT SELECT ON Patients TO PatientDataRole
```

5. Click **Query -> Connection -> Change Connection**.

6. Select **SQL Server Authentication**.

7. Log in using PatientUser with the password P@tientPassword2.

8. Execute the following query:

```
SELECT * FROM Patients
```

Question 2: What happened?

9. Make sure you have only a single query window open.

10. Execute the following statements

```
EXEC sp_setapprole'PatientDataRole','P@t1ent';

SELECT*FROM Patients WHERE PatientKey ='1-24'
```

NOTE: If you have more than one query window open, you will receive an error in the message window that sp_setapprole was not called correctly. In fact, it did execute. The error results because you are running the statement from within a query window that is sharing a connection with other query windows.

1. Click the **Results** tab and verify that the data was selected from the table.

2. Take a screenshot and save it as nnLab9-1Step7. Turn in the two screenshots along with your Word document.

Lab 9.2 (Group B)—Manage Logins and Roles

> **Critical Review**
> * You can use server-level roles to assign permission to perform server administration tasks.
> * You can use fixed database-level roles to assign permissions to administer and access a database.
> * You can use the ALTER LOGIN statement to modify a login or unlock a locked login.
> * You can create an application role that is not associated with a specific database user. * A full backup backs up the entire database.
> * A transaction log backup backs up only the transaction log.

Step 1: Create a login named DatabaseAdmin with the password DB&dmin.

Step 2: Add DatabaseAdmin to the dbcreator server-level role.

Step 3: Create a user named DBUser in the Westlake database.

Step 4: Make DBUser a member of the db_backupoperator fixed database role.

Step 5: Make DBUser a member of the db_ddladmin fixed database role.

Step 6: Create a user named DBUser in the GrandfieldCollege database.

Step 7: Make DBUser a member of the db_backupoperator fixed database role.

Step 8: Make DBUser a member of the db_ddladmin fixed database role.

Step 9: Take screenshots to turn in:

1. Expand **Security**. Expand **Logins**.
2. Right-click **DatabaseAdmin** and choose **Properties**.
3. Take a screenshot of the Server Roles tab and save it as *nn*Lab9-2_3.
4. Take a screenshot of the **User Mappings** tab and save it as *nn*Lab9-2_4.
5. Expand **Databases->Westlake->Security->Users**.
6. Right-click **DBAdmin** and choose **Properties**.
7. Take a screenshot of the **General** tab and save it as *nn*Lab9-2_7.
8. Turn in all three screenshots.

Course Project

Critical Review

- You can create a table using the CREATE TABLE command or by right-clicking the **Tables** folder and running **New Table**.
- You can use Database Diagrams to create a relationship.
- You can add a column to a table by right-clicking the table and choosing **Design**.
- You can use the following data modification language (DML) statements to modify the data in a table:
  - INSERT—add a new row
  - UPDATE—modify a row
  - DELETE—delete a row
- You can create a trigger to cause an action to occur either after or instead of a DML statement.
- You can use stored procedures to guard against SQL injection attacks.
- A SQL injection attack adds malicious code to a SQL statement that is dynamically constructed.
- Stored procedures help protect against SQL injection because:
  - The query only accepts values of the data type specified in the parameter.
  - Multiple statements are not executed as a batch.
- You can use grant permissions to perform an action to database roles, application roles, or users.
- You can create an index to optimize performance.
- You can use a SELECT statement to retrieve data. It supports the following clauses
  - FROM—identify the table
  - ORDER BY—sort the data
  - WHERE – filter the data
    - LIKE—retrieve data that matches a pattern
    - =, <, >—retrieve data that meets a condition
    - BETWEEN—retrieve data in a range
  - JOIN—join two tables together
  - GROUP BY—group aggregated data
- The GetDate function retrieves the current date.

Step 1: Launch the VMware Player and play the SQL2008ExpVM virtual machine stored on your USB drive.

Step 2: Open a Word document on the host computer and save it as *nn*Projectanswers. You will be asked questions during the course project and document the answers in the Word document. This is the file you will turn in to your instructor.

Step 3: On the virtual machine, open SQL Server Management Studio and connect to the SQL Server Express instance.

Step 4: In the Westlake database, create a table named PatientVisits that includes the columns defined here:

	Column Name	Data Type	Allow Nulls
🔑	PatientKey	nchar(15)	☐
🔑	VisitDate	date	☐
	BloodPressure	nchar(8)	☐
	Weight	decimal(18, 0)	☐
	Pulse	int	☐
	DepressionLevel	int	☐
	DoctorNotes	varchar(MAX)	☑

To create a composite key:

1. Click **PatientKey**.

2. Hold down the **SHIFT** key and select **VisitDate**.

3. Right-click the key column in the highlighted region and choose **Set Primary Key**.

Step 5: Create a PatientVisitSymptoms table that includes the columns defined here:

	Column Name	Data Type	Allow Nulls
🔑	PatientKey	nchar(15)	☐
🔑	VisitDate	date	☐
	Symptom	varchar(100)	☐
▶			☐

Step 6: Use the Database Diagram to specify the relationships shown below:

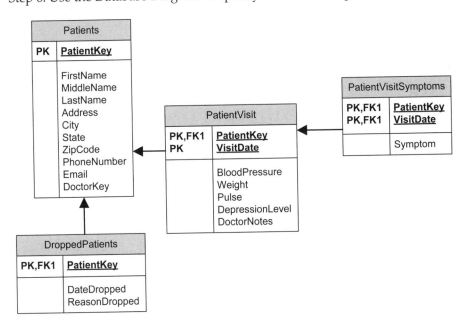

1. Expand Database Diagrams.
2. Double-click the dbo.WestlakeDiagram.
3. Right-click in an empty area and choose **Add Table**.
4. Select both tables and click **Add**.
5. Move the tables and draw the relationships to match those shown above. When defining the relationship between PatientVisitSymptoms and PatientVisit, make sure the Tables and Columns dialog looks like this:

Tables and Columns   [?][X]

Relationship name:

FK_PatientVisitSymptoms_PatientVisits

Primary key table:	Foreign key table:
PatientVisits	PatientVisitSymptoms
PatientKey	PatientKey
VisitDate	VisitDate

OK   Cancel

6. Take a screenshot and save it as nnProject_6 to submit to your instructor as part of the project deliverables.
7. Close the Database Diagram. Make sure to save your changes.

Step 7: Create a stored procedure name RecordPatientVisit that inserts data into the PatientVisits table. Creating a stored procedure helps protect against a SQL injection attack.

1. Think about a program that executed a dynamic query to insert records into the PatientVisits table:

```
"INSERT INTOPatientVisits (PatientKey, VisitDate, BloodPressure,
Weight, Pulse, DepressionLevel, DoctorNotes) VALUES (" +
patientkey + ", " + visitdate + ", " + bp + ", " + weight +", "
+ pulse + ", " + level + ", " + notes + ");"
```

A malicious user could set the notes variable as follows:

notes = "); DELETE * from Patients; '"

If that happened, the INSERT statement would execute and then the DELETE statement would execute and all data would be deleted from the Patients table, provided the user had DELETE permission on the Patients table.

To guard against such an attack, you can create a stored procedure that encapsulates the INSERT statement.

2. Right-click the **PatientVisits** table and choose **Script table as -> INSERT to -> New Query Editor Window**.

3. Modify the statement to look like the one below and execute it.

```
CREATE PROCEDURE usp_RecordPatientVisit @PatientKey nchar(15)
,@VisitDate date
,@BloodPressure nchar(8)
,@Weight decimal(18,0)
,@Pulse int
,@DepressionLevel int
,@DoctorNotes varchar(max)
AS
INSERT INTO [Westlake].[dbo].[PatientVisits]
([PatientKey]
,[VisitDate]
,[BloodPressure]
,[Weight]
,[Pulse]
,[DepressionLevel]
,[DoctorNotes])
VALUES
        (@PatientKey,
        @VisitDate, @BloodPressure, @Weight, @Pulse,
        @DepressionLevel, @DoctorNotes)
GO
```

Step 8: Use similar steps to those performed in step 7 to create a stored procedure named RecordPatientSymptoms that inserts data into the PatientVisitSymptoms table.

Step 9: Grant the DoctorsRole the Execute permission on both RecordPatientVisit and RecordPatientSymptoms.

Step 10: Open ProjectLoadData.sql. Copy the contents to the query window and execute. If you get an error, make sure you created the stored procedures correctly.

Step 11: Explore the clustered index on the PatientVisits table.

1. Execute the following statement:

   SELECT*FROM PatientVisits

2. Take a screen capture of the results and save it as *nn*Project_11_2.

3. Expand **PatientVisits->Indexes**.

4. Double-click the clustered index.

   Question 1: Which sort order is determined by the current index?

   Question 2: How does this relate to the sort order returned by the query?

Step 12: Create a non-clustered index on the DepressionLevel column of **PatientVisits**.

1. Right-click **Index** and choose **New Index**.
2. Configure the index as shown below:

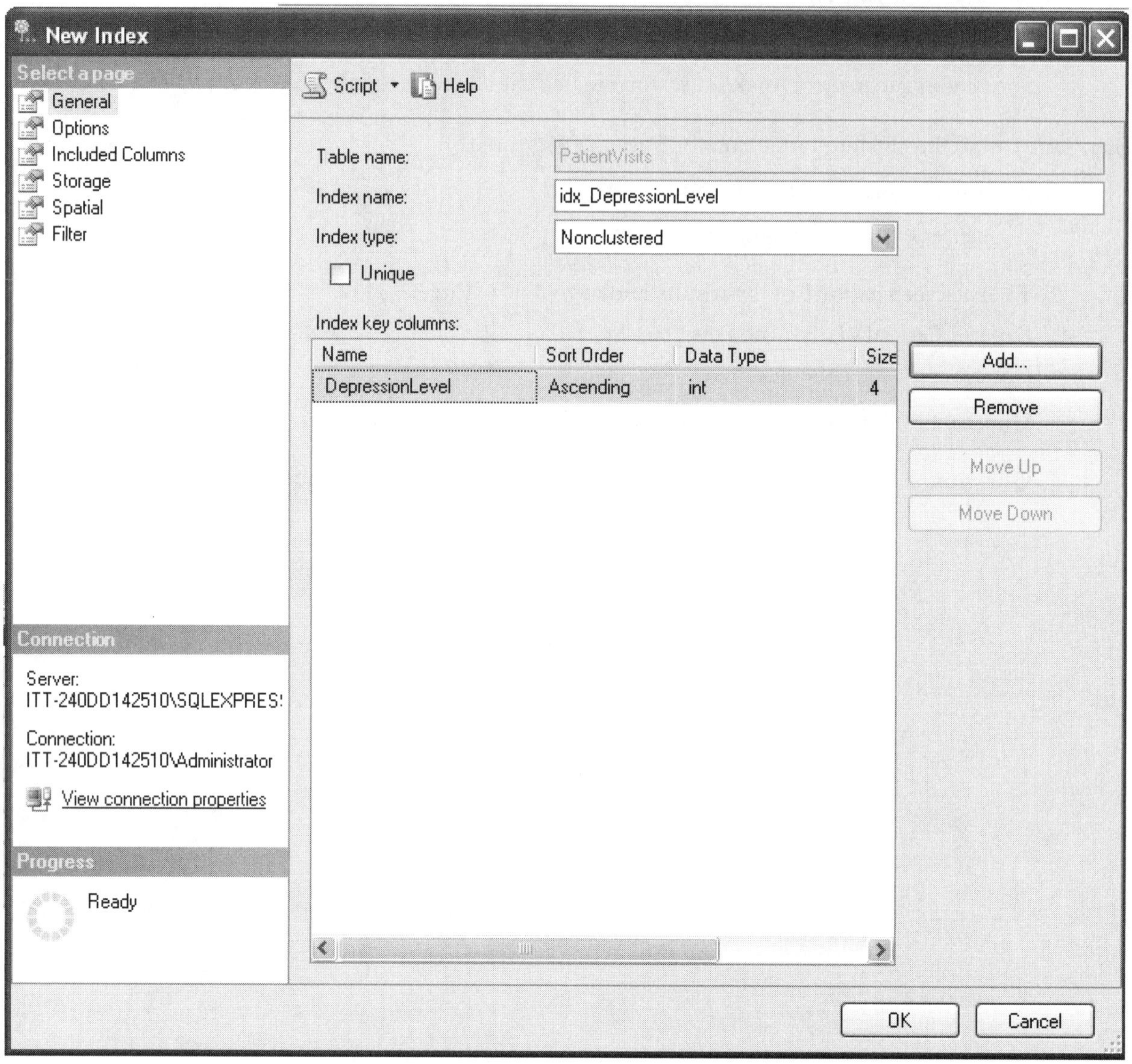

3. Click **OK**.
4. Execute the query:

```
SELECT*FROM PatientVisits
```

Question 3: Did the sort order change? Why or why not?

Step 13: Create a trigger that logs the date and time of an update to the Patients table.

1. Right-click the **Patients** table and choose **Design**.

2. Add a ModifiedDate column as shown below.

	Column Name	Data Type	Allow Nulls
🔑	PatientKey	nchar(15)	☐
	DoctorKey	nchar(15)	☐
	FirstName	varchar(25)	☐
	MiddleName	varchar(25)	☑
	LastName	varchar(25)	☐
	PhoneNumber	nchar(20)	☑
▶	DateModified	datetime	☑

3. Click File -> Save Patients.

4. Expand Patients.

5. Right-click Triggers and choose New Trigger.

6. Modify the trigger code to perform an UPDATE that logs the current date to the ModifiedDate column after an UPDATE occurs. HINT: Use the Inserted table to determine which patient's record was modified.

7. Execute the following statement:

```
UPDATE Patients SET PhoneNumber ='555-2222'
WHERE PatientKey ='5-13'
```

9. Execute the following statement:

```
SELECT * FROM Patients
```

9. Take a screenshot and name it *nn*Project_13.

Step 14: Execute queries to meet the following requirements. For each query, take a screen shot and save it for submission.

1. Execute a query that retrieves the visit date and patient key for all patients that reported a depression level over 5. Save the screenshot as *nn*Project_14_1.

2. Execute a query that retrieves the visit date and patient name, and depression level for all patients that reported a depression level over 5. Your results should be formatted as follows:

	VisitDate	Patient	DepressionLevel
1	2012-09-07	Sally Johnson	6
2	2012-08-15	Susan Michaels	6
3	2012-08-01	Susan Michaels	8

Save the screenshot as *nn*Project_14_2.

3. Execute a query that retrieves the number of patient visits that occurred in which the patient had a pulse over 45. Save the screenshot as *nn*Project_14_3.

4. Execute a query that lists the visit date and patient name for each patient visit, sorted by depression level from lowest to highest. Format the patient's name as in 14.2. Save the screenshot as *nn*Project_14_4.

5. Execute a query that displays the patient's last name, average pulse and average depression level for each patient. Save the screenshot as *nn*Project14_5.

Step 15: Turn in your Word document and all screen shots.